IDENTIFYING

DOG BREEDS

The new compact study guide and identifier

DOG BREEDS

The new compact study guide and identifier

Joan Palmer

CHARTWELL
BOOKS, INC.

A QUINTET BOOK

Published by Chartwell Books
A Division of Book Sales, Inc.
PO Box 7100
Edison, New Jersey 08818-7100

This edition for sale in the U.S.A., its
territories and dependencies only.

ISBN 0-7858-0326-2

This book was designed and produced by
Quintet Publishing Limited
6 Blundell Street
London N7 9BH

Creative Director: Richard Dewing
Designers: Bob Mathias and Jervis Tuttell
Project Editor: Claire Tennant-Scull
Editor: Katie Preston
Photographer: Paul Forrester

Manufactured in Singapore by J Film
Printed in Singapore by Star Standard
Industries (Pte) Ltd

CONTENTS

INTRODUCTION

People have known for more than 2,000 years that, by selective breeding, they could produce dogs that were not only a desired colour and size, but which had inbred characteristics, for example strong guarding instincts or keen eyesight. Now you can learn to recognize the different physical and mental characteristics of over 100 dog breeds with this superb illustrated guide.

Formation and Terminology
A special vocabulary has been developed to standardize the way in which the world's breeds are described.

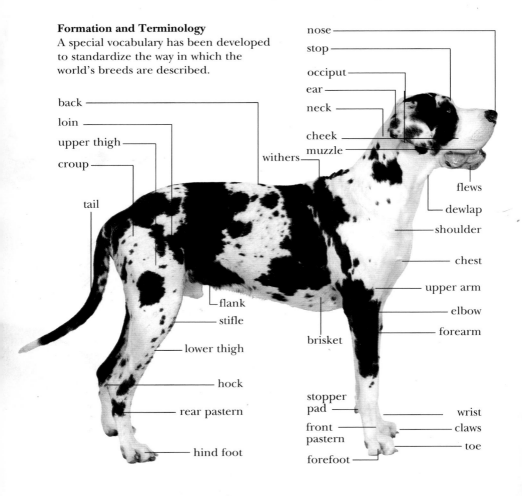

nose
stop
occiput
ear
neck
cheek
muzzle
withers
flews
dewlap
shoulder
chest
upper arm
elbow
forearm
back
loin
upper thigh
croup
tail
flank
stifle
lower thigh
hock
rear pastern
hind foot
brisket
stopper pad
front pastern
forefoot
wrist
claws
toe

HEADS

There are three basic skull types, which are further divided into sub-types. Eight typical sub-types, featured in the Dog Identifier section, are illustrated below. Heads lacking in refinement are termed "coarse".

Apple

Balanced

Blocky

Clean

Egg-shaped

Otter

Pear

Rectangular

EARS

A dog's ears are described in terms of their shape and how they hang from the head. The phrase "set on" refers to the position of the ears in relation to eye level and/or the width of the skull. Nine standard ear types are illustrated.

Bat

Button

EARS
(continued)

Drop

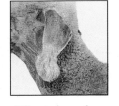

Filbert-shaped

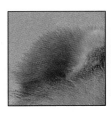

Hooded

Hound

Pricked

Rose

Semi-drop

TAILS

The names given to tails refer to their length, shape, position and the hair covering them. The "tail set" refers to the way in which its base is set on the rump; whereas how the tail is "set on" refers to it placement – high, low and so

Bobtail

Flag

Kink

Otter

Screw

Sickle

Spike

Stern

COLOURS

Belton

Blue

Brindle

Grizzle

Harlequin

Piebald

Red

Roan

Tricolour

Wheaten

on. About 45 breeds in total have docked, or shortened, tails. The operation is performed by a veterinary surgeon.

Ring

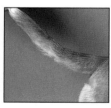
Sabre

Squirrel

Whip

HOW TO USE THIS BOOK

The breeds are arranged in groups – utility dogs, working dogs, gundogs, hounds, terriers and toy dogs. Within each group the dogs are arranged by country of origin moving, from North America, west to east around the globe.

KEY TO SYMBOLS

These symbols provide at-a-glance information on how much care a breed requires. The four categories – food, grooming, space and exercise – are divided into four grades. Within the exercise category for example, one quarter shaded indicates little exercise is required, total shading indicates the need for a great deal of exercise.

Food

Grooming

Space

Exercise

OLD ENGLISH BULLDOG

An ancient breed, the Bulldog was developed for bull-baiting around the 13th century.

COAT Short, smooth and close.
COLOUR Uniform colour or with black mask or muzzle; red, red brindle, piebald; black undesirable in show dogs.
FEATURES Large skull; eyes set low; ears small and set high on head; broad, sloping shoulders; tail set low and can be either straight or screwed.
SIZE Height: 31–36cm (12–14in). Weight: dogs 23–25kg (50–55lb), bitches 18–23kg (40–50lb).
CARE Needs daily brushing and a rub-down. Do not exert in hot weather.
CHARACTER Gentle and good-natured.

BOSTON TERRIER

Derived from a crossbred Bulldog/Terrier, the Boston was imported into the US in the 19th century.

COAT Short and smooth.
COLOUR Brindle with white markings and black with white markings.
FEATURES Compactly built and well balanced. Square head, flat on top; round eyes set wide apart; broad, square jaw; ears erect at corners of head; broad chest; fine, low-set tail.
SIZE Height: 38–43cm (15–17in). Weight not exceeding 11.5kg (25lb).
CARE Easy to look after, requires little grooming.
CHARACTER Lively, intelligent, but determined and self-willed.

DALMATIAN

Named after Dalmatia on the Adriatic coast, the Dalmatian was established in Britain, where it was popular as a carriage dog in the 1800s.

COAT Short, fine, dense and close; sleek and glossy in appearance.
COLOUR Pure white ground colour with black or liver-brown spots. Spots on extremities smaller than those on body.
FEATURES Long head and flat skull; eyes set moderately far apart; medium-sized ears set high; deep chest; long tail that is carried with a slight upward curve.
SIZE Height at withers: 48–58cm (19–23in). Weight: 23–25kg (50–55lb).
CARE Requires plenty of exercise and daily brushing; tends to shed white hairs.
CHARACTER Affectionate and energetic. Intelligent and equable temperament.

FRENCH BULLDOG

A descendant of small bulldogs, but not certain whether they originated from Spanish or English stock, the French Bulldog became a popular breed at the turn of the century.

COAT Short, smooth and finely textured.
COLOUR Brindle, pied or fawn.
FEATURES Head square, large and broad; eyes dark and set wide apart; distinctive "bat ears", set high and carried upright; body short, muscular and cobby; tail very short, though not docked.
SIZE Height: 30cm (12in). Weight: dogs about 12.5kg (28lb), bitches 11kg (24lb).
CARE Daily brush and rub-down needed to make the coat shine. Facial creases need lubrication to prevent soreness.
CHARACTER Gentle, good-natured, affectionate and courageous.

STANDARD SCHNAUZER

The Standard is the oldest of the three varieties of Schnauzer. The breed's origins are not certain, though it is thought to be descended from cattle dogs and it is at least 500 years old.

COAT Harsh, hardy and wiry.
COLOUR Pure black (white markings on head, chest and legs undesirable in show dogs) or pepper and salt.
FEATURES Strong head of a good length; dark, oval-shaped eyes; neat, pointed ears, chest moderately broad; tail is set on and carried high, and is characteristically docked to three joints.

SIZE Height at shoulders: dogs 46–49cm (18–19$\frac{1}{2}$in), bitches 44–46cm (17$\frac{1}{2}$–18in). Weight: around 15kg (33lb).
CARE Needs plenty of exercise and the wiry coats need a certain amount of stripping and plucking - get advice from your breeder or take to a local grooming parlour before tackling this type of grooming. Pet dogs, can be clipped.
CHARACTER Attractive, robust, intelligent and playful.

GIANT SCHNAUZER

Originally a cattle dog, the Giant Schnauzer, or Riesenschnauzer, was in danger of extinction until it proved its worth as a guard dog during the First World War.

COAT Harsh, hardy and wiry.
COLOUR Pure black or pepper and salt.
FEATURES Strong head of a good length; dark, oval-shaped eyes; neat, pointed ears, chest moderately broad; tail is set on and carried high, and is characteristically docked to three joints.
SIZE Height at shoulders: dogs 65–70cm (25$^1/_2$–27$^1/_2$in), bitches 60–65cm (23$^1/_2$–25$^1/_2$in). Weight: about 33–35kg (73–77lb).
CARE Needs little grooming other than stripping and plucking.
CHARACTER Intelligent, reliable, good-natured.

MINIATURE SCHNAUZER

Known in its native Germany as the Zwergschnauzer, this breed was derived from crossing the Standard Schnauzer with smaller dogs – probably Affenpinschers.

COAT Harsh, hardy and wiry.
COLOUR Pure black or pepper and salt.
FEATURES Strong head of a good length; dark, oval-shaped eyes; neat, pointed ears, tail is set on and carried high, and is normally docked to three joints.
SIZE Height at shoulders: 30–35cm (12–14in). Weight: about 6–7kg (13–15lb).
CARE Needs a fair amount of exercise; coat needs periodic plucking and stripping and whiskers should be combed every day.
CHARACTER Lively and friendly; makes an excellent family pet.

STANDARD POODLE

**Known in France as the Caniche,
the Poodle was favoured by the
French Queen Marie Antoinette
(1755–93). However it
originated in Germany as a
water retriever or *pudel*. It
resembles the Irish Water
Spaniel – they have a common
ancestor in the French Barbet.**

COAT Very profuse and dense; a
good, harsh texture
COLOUR All solid colours, clear
colours preferred for showing.
FEATURES Long, fine head; almond-
shaped eyes; ears set on high and
hanging close to head; chest deep
and broad; tail set on high and
carried up.
SIZE Height at shoulders: over
38cm (15in). Weight: 20–32kg
(45–70lb).
CARE Coat needs clipping every six
weeks and you will need a wire-pin
pneumatic brush and a wire-toothed
metal comb for daily grooming. The
lion clip, shown here, is obligatory for
show dogs although many pet owners
prefer the lamb clip, with the hair a
uniform length. Poodles do not moult
and so their coat does not affect
asthma sufferers.
CHARACTER Happy, good-tempered and
lively; intelligent and eager to learn –
makes a good obedience dog.

MINIATURE POODLE

Bred down from the Standard, by using smaller specimens, this breed hit its peak of popularity in the 1950s.

COAT Very profuse and dense.
COLOUR All solid colours, clear colours preferred in show dogs.
FEATURES Long, fine head; almond-shaped eyes; ears set on high and hanging close to head; chest deep and broad; tail set on high and carried up.
SIZE Height at shoulders: 25–38cm (10–15in). Weight: 12–14kg (26–31lb).
CARE Miniature poodles also require daily grooming with wire-pin pneumatic brush and a wire-toothed metal comb.

CHARACTER Intelligent and fun-loving.

TOY POODLE

Bred down from the Standard, Toy Poodles were made a separate breed in the 1950s.

COAT Very profuse and dense; a harsh texture.
COLOUR All solid colours, clear colours preferred.
FEATURES Long, fine head; almond-shaped eyes; ears set on high; chest deep and broad; tail set on high and carried up.
SIZE Height at shoulders: under 25cm (10in). Weight: 7kg (15lb).

CARE Like the Miniature and Standard, the Toy Poodle's coat requires daily grooming and clipping every six weeks.
CHARACTER Ideal for an apartment. The least robust of the three types.

CHOW CHOW

A member of the spitz family, the Chow Chow has been known in its native China for more than 2,000 years. It is the only breed with a black tongue.

COAT Can be rough – abundant, dense and coarse with pronounced ruff and feathering on tail, or smooth – dense and hard with no ruff or feathering.
COLOUR Black, red, blue, fawn and cream.
FEATURES Broad, flat head; small ears slightly rounded at tips; broad, deep chest and compact body; tail set on high and carried curled over the back.
SIZE Height at shoulders: dogs 48–56cm (19–22in), bitches 46–51cm (18–20in). Weight 20–32kg (44–70lb).
CARE The coat needs considerable attention with a wire brush.
CHARACTER Faithful, alert, independent.

LHASA APSO

This breed originated in Tibet and may be descended from the Tibetan Mastiff.

COAT Top coat long, heavy, straight and hard. Moderate undercoat.
COLOUR Solid golden, sandy, honey, dark grizzle, slate or smoke; black parti-colour, white or brown.
FEATURES Long hair on head covering eyes and reaching towards floor; heavily feathered ears; dark eyes; compact, well-balanced body; tail set on high and carried over the back.
SIZE Height at shoulders: dogs about 25cm (10in), bitches slightly smaller. Weight: 6–7kg (13–15lb).
CARE The long coat needs careful daily grooming.
CHARACTER Happy, usually long-lived and adaptable.

JAPANESE SPITZ

The Japanese Spitz shares an ancestor with the Nordic Spitz and is also closely related to the German Spitz and the Pomeranian.

COAT Straight, dense, stand-off outer coat; thick, short dense undercoat.
COLOUR Pure white.
FEATURES Medium-sized head; dark eyes; small, triangular, erect ears; broad, deep chest; tail set on high and carried curled over its back; black nose.
SIZE Height at shoulders: dogs 30–36cm (12–14in), bitches slightly smaller. Average weight: 6kg (13lb).
CARE Needs daily brushing and a fair amount of exercise.
CHARACTER Loyal to its owners but distrustful of strangers; intelligent, lively and bold – makes a fine small guard dog and a good companion.

SHIBA INU

The Shiba Inu is an ancient Japanese breed – remains of a dog of this type were found in ruins dating back to 500BC. It is the smallest of the spitz types and its name means "little dog" in the Nagano dialect.

COAT Harsh and straight, but luxuriant.
COLOUR Red, salt and pepper, black, black and tan, or white.
FEATURES Agile, sturdily built and well muscled; deep chest; long back; almond-shaped eyes; long sickle tail.
SIZE Height at shoulders: dogs 38–40cm (15–16in), bitches 35–38cm (14–15in). Weight 9–13.5kg (20–30lb).
CARE Needs a fair amount of exercise and a good daily brushing.
CHARACTER Affectionate, friendly and sensitive, but sometimes aloof. A good hunter, pet or show dog.

SHAR-PEI

At one time the rarest dog in the world, the Shar-Pei, or Chinese Fighting Dog, dates back to the Han Dynasty (206BC–AD220).

COAT Short, straight and bristly.
COLOUR Solid colours only – black, red, light or dark fawn or cream.
FEATURES Loose skin. Head rather large in proportion to body; dark, almond-shaped eyes; very small, triangular ears; broad, deep chest; rounded tail narrowing to a fine point, set on high

and curling over to one side.
SIZE Height at withers: 46–51cm ($18^1/_2$–20in). Weight: 18–25kg (40–55lb).
CARE The Shar-Pei's coat is never trimmed. It does need a fair amount of exercise.
CHARACTER Very affectionate dog, despite its frowning expression; calm, independent and devoted.

TIBETAN TERRIER

The Tibetan Terrier is not really a terrier at all, having no history of going to earth. It resembles a small Old English Sheepdog and is said to have been bred in Tibetan monasteries for farm work and as a companion.

COAT Soft, woolly undercoat; long, fine outer coat that can be straight or wavy.
COLOUR Any colour or combination of colours.
FEATURES Large round, dark eyes; pendant, feathered ears; compact and powerful body; medium-length tail set quite high and curled over the back.
SIZE Height at shoulders: dogs 35–40cm (14–16in), bitches slightly smaller. Weight 9–11kg (20–24lb).
CARE The Tibetan Terrier's long coat needs regular attention.
CHARACTER Loyal, sturdy, a good walker and devoted to its owners.

NEWFOUNDLAND

With its instinct to retrieve anything, or anyone, in the water, the Newfoundland is famous as a life-saver.

COAT Oily, water-resistant double coat that is flat, dense and coarse textured.
COLOUR Black, brown, grey or Landseer (black head, black markings on white).
FEATURES Massive, broad head; small, dark brown eyes; small ears set well back; strong, broad, muscular body; thick tail.
SIZE Height at shoulders: dogs 71cm (28in), bitches 66cm (26in). Weight: dogs 64–69kg (140–152lb), bitches 50–54kg (110–120lb).
CARE Needs daily brushing.
CHARACTER Gentle, good-tempered.

MASTIFF

One of the most ancient breeds, Mastiff-like dogs were treasured by the Babylonians over 4,000 years ago.

COAT Outer coat short and straight; undercoat dense and close-lying.
COLOUR Apricot, fawn or brindle. Muzzle should be black.
FEATURES Broad skull; small eyes set wide apart; small ears; long, broad body; legs squarely set; tail set on high.
SIZE Minimum height: dogs 75cm (30in), bitches 69cm ($27\frac{1}{2}$in). Weight: 79–86kg (174–190lb).
CARE Needs regular walking to build up its muscles. Many do not complete their growth until their second year.
CHARACTER Alert and loyal.

BULLMASTIFF

The Bullmastiff was developed 200–300 years ago by crossing the Mastiff with the British Bulldog to create a powerful, brave fighting dog.

COAT Short, smooth and dense.
COLOUR Any shade of brindle, fawn or red; black muzzle.
FEATURES Large, square head; dark or hazel-coloured eyes; V-shaped ears set high and wide apart; strong, compact body; tail set on high.
SIZE Height at shoulders: dogs 64–68cm (25–27in), bitches 60–66cm (24–26in). Weight: dogs 50–60kg (110–130lb), bitches 41–50kg (90–110lb).
CARE Needs plenty of space and exercise, but only needs grooming every few days.
CHARACTER Playful, loyal, gentle; should only be kept by experienced owners.

BOXER

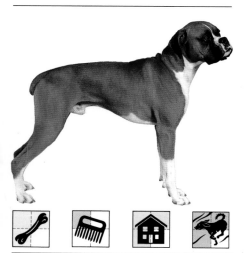

The Boxer can be traced back to the mastiff-type dogs taken into battle against the Romans by the Cimbrians.

COAT Short, glossy and smooth.
COLOUR Fawn or brindle with white markings. For showing, the white should not make up more than one third of the ground colour.
FEATURES Dark brown, forward-looking eyes; moderate-sized ears set wide apart; body square in profile; tail set on high and characteristically docked.
SIZE Height: dogs 57–64cm (22 1/2 –25in), bitches 53–58cm (21–23in). Weight: 24–32kg (53–71lb).
CARE Boxers need a fair amount of exercise, but the coat is easy to care for.
CHARACTER Affectionate and playful, but not averse to a scrap with other dogs.

SMOOTH COLLIE

The ancestors of both Rough and Smooth Collies were brought over from Iceland to Scotland over 400 years ago, where they were used as sheepdogs – the word "colley" is a Scottish term for a sheep with a black face and legs.

COAT Short, harsh and smooth with a dense undercoat.

COLOUR Sable and white, tricolour, blue merle. (Blue merles are not allowed in the UK show ring.)

FEATURES Head should appear light in proportion to body; almond-shaped eyes; ears small and not too close together;

body slightly long in relation to height; long tail usually carried low.

SIZE Height at shoulders: dogs 56–66cm (22–26in), bitches 51–60cm (20–24in). Weight: dogs 20.5–34kg (45–75lb), bitches 18–29.5kg (40–65lb).

CARE Needs plenty of space and exercise. The coat is not difficult to groom.

CHARACTERS Loyal, affectionate, easy to train; naturally suspicious of strangers and makes an excellent guard dog.

ROUGH COLLIE

The Rough Collie, sometimes called the Scots or Scottish Collie, is still best known as the star of the "Lassie" films. Identical to the Smooth Collie, the Rough Collie is much more common.

COAT Very dense, straight outer coat harsh to touch, with soft, furry, very close undercoat.
COLOUR Sable and white, tricolour, blue merle, which is not permissible when showing in the UK.
FEATURES Head should appear light in proportion to body; medium-sized, almond-shaped eyes; ears small and not too close together; body slightly long in relation to height; long tail.
SIZE Height at shoulders: dogs 56–65cm (22–25½in), bitches 51–60cm (20–24in). Weight: dogs 20.5–34kg (45–75lb), bitches 18–29.5kg (40–65lb).
CARE Needs plenty of exercise and space but is not difficult to groom.
CHARACTER Intelligent, hardy, has keen eyesight. They are easy to train and make good guard dogs.

SHETLAND SHEEPDOG

The "Sheltie" originated in the Shetlands off the north coast of Scotland, where it has bred true for more than 135 years.

COAT Outer coat of long, harsh-textured hair; soft, short-haired, close undercoat.
COLOUR Sable, tricolour, blue merle, black and white, and black and tan.
FEATURES Refined head, with medium-sized, almond-shaped eyes, obliquely set; ears small and moderately wide at base; muscular, arched neck; back level; tail set low and tapering towards tip.
SIZE Height at withers: dogs about 37cm ($14^{1}/_{2}$in), bitches about 35cm (14in). Weight: 6–7kg (13–15lb).
CARE Requires daily grooming using a stiff-bristled brush and a comb. Should not be kennelled outside.
CHARACTER An intelligent, faithful dog that enjoys exercise.

OLD ENGLISH SHEEPDOG

Old English Sheepdogs, or "Bobtails", have existed for centuries. They were once used as cattle dogs and guards, but are now almost exclusively pet dogs.

COAT Profuse but not excessive, and a good harsh texture.
COLOUR Any shade of grey, grizzle or blue.
FEATURES Head in proportion to body; eyes set well apart; small ears carried flat to the side of the head; short, compact body; tail docked close to body.
SIZE Height at withers: dogs 56cm (22in), bitches 53cm (21in). Minimum weight: 30kg (66lb).
CARE Pet dogs need daily brushing. Show dogs require many hours of grooming.
CHARACTER Good-natured, devoted and sensible, but boisterous.

BEARDED COLLIE

BORDER COLLIE

Descended from Polish Lowland Sheepdogs, the Bearded Collie is believed to be one of the oldest herding dogs in Scotland.

COAT Flat, harsh and shaggy; can be slightly wavy; soft, furry, close undercoat.
COLOUR Slate grey, reddish fawn, black, blue, all shades of grey, brown or sandy, with or without white markings.
FEATURES Broad, flat head; medium-sized, drooping ears; long body; tail set low, without a kink or twist.
SIZE Height at withers: dogs 53–56cm (21–22in), bitches 51–53cm (20–21in). Weight: 18–27kg (40–60lb).
CARE Needs careful grooming to prevent moulting.
CHARACTER Alert, self-confident and active dog. Makes a good pet and show dog.

The Border Collie is a descendant of working collies from the border between Scotland and England. It has taken part in sheepdog trials since 1873.

COAT Two varieties: moderately long, and smooth; both are thick, straight coats.
COLOUR Variety of colours. For showing, white should never predominate.
FEATURES Oval-shaped eyes set wide apart; medium-sized ears set wide apart; body athletic in appearance; tail moderately long.
SIZE Height: dogs 53cm (21in), bitches slightly less. Weight: 13.5–20kg (30–45lb).
CARE Needs a great deal of exercise and regular grooming with a brush and comb.
CHARACTER A hardy, highly intelligent and loyal dog. Also has a natural instinct to herd.

CORGI (PEMBROKE)

The Welsh Corgi Pembroke, a favourite of British royalty, has been a working dog in South Wales since the 11th century – its job was to control the movement of cattle by nipping their legs. It may be descended from the Swedish Vallhund.

COAT Medium length and straight, with a dense undercoat.
COLOUR Red, sable, fawn or black and tan, with or without white markings on legs, brisket and neck.
FEATURES Foxy head; upright, slightly rounded ears; deep chest and moderately long body; short tail, docked if necessary.
SIZE Height at shoulders: 25–30cm (10–12in). Weight: dogs about 12kg (27lb), bitches about 11.5kg (25lb).
CARE Tends to put on weight if under-exercised. Coat needs daily brushing.
CHARACTER Extremely active and devoted little dogs.

CORGI (CARDIGAN)

The Welsh Corgi Cardigan has a similar history to the more popular Pembroke and, until the 1930s, the two breeds were inter-bred. The Cardigan is heavier boned and larger bodied and is easily distinguished from the Pembroke by its long, bushy tail.

COAT Short or medium length, with a hard texture; short, thick undercoat.
COLOUR Any, with or without white markings. White should not predominate.
FEATURES Foxy head; medium-sized eyes; upright ears; broad chest with prominent breast bone; bushy tail, in line with body.
SIZE Height at withers: 26–31cm (10$\frac{1}{2}$–12$\frac{1}{2}$in). Weight: dogs 13.5–17kg (30–38lb), bitches 11.5–15.5kg (25–34lb).
CARE Tendency to put on weight if under-exercised. The water-resistant coat needs daily brushing.
CHARACTER Active and devoted. Said to have a slightly more equable temperament than the Pembroke.

BELGIAN SHEPHERD DOG

The long-haired Tervueren, named after its region of origin, was developed by a local breeder.

All four varieties (Groenendael, Malinois, Tervueren, and Laekenois) were developed from the many sheepdogs found in Belgium in the late 1800s. They are regarded as separate breeds everywhere except the UK.

COAT Groenendael and Tervueren: long, straight and abundant. Malinois: very short on head, ears and lower legs, short on body. Laekenois: harsh and wiry.
COLOUR Groenendael: black, black with moderate white. Tervueren: all shades of red, fawn, grey, with black overlap. Malinois: all shades of red, fawn, grey , with black overlap. Laekenois: reddish fawn with black shading.
FEATURES Finely chiselled head; medium-sized eyes; triangular ears; powerful but elegant body, broad-chested; medium-length tail, firmly set on.
SIZE Height: dogs 61–66cm (24–26in), bitches 56–61cm (22–24in). Weight: 28kg (62lb).
CARE Needs plenty of exercise and regular grooming.
CHARACTER Intelligent and attentive and make good guard and obedience dogs.

PYRENEAN MOUNTAIN DOG

Also known as the Great Pyrenees, this breed probably originated in Asia.

COAT Long and coarse-textured, with a profuse, fine undercoat .
COLOUR White, with patches of badger, and wolf-grey or yellow.
FEATURES Rounded crown; small, triangular ears; broad chest; level back; tapering tail.
SIZE Height at withers: dogs 70–80cm (28–32in), bitches 66–73cm (25½–28in). Weight: 40–50kg (88–110lb).
CARE Can be kept in or out of doors, but must be well trained.
CHARACTER Good-natured, gets on with other pets and is a faithful protector.

SAINT BERNARD

Named after a medieval Hospice in the Swiss Alps, the Saint Bernard became famous for mountain search and rescue.

COAT Dense, short and smooth.
COLOUR Orange, mahogany-brindle, red-brindle or white, with coloured patches on body; white blaze on face, white on muzzle, collar, chest, forelegs, feet and end of tail; black on face and ears.
FEATURES Massive head; muscular shoulders; broad, straight back; tail set on high.
SIZE Height: 61–71cm (24–28in). Weight: 50–91kg (110–200lb).
CARE Should not be given too much exercise in its first year. Needs daily brushing.
CHARACTER Intelligent, very trainable, loves children and is very kind.

BERNESE MOUNTAIN DOG

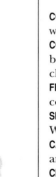

Named after Berne, Switzerland, this breed is believed to be descended from the ancient Molossus dog.

COAT Thick and straight or slightly wavy, with a bright, natural sheen.
COLOUR Jet black, with rich, reddish-brown markings; white markings on head, chest, tip of tail and feet.
FEATURES Strong head with a flat skull; compact body; bushy tail.
SIZE Height: 58–70cm (23–27$\frac{1}{2}$in). Weight: about 40kg (88lb).
CARE Needs plenty of space and exercise and regular brushing.
CHARACTER A gentle, amiable dog that makes a loyal and affectionate pet.

DOBERMAN

The Doberman was developed in the 1880s in Germany from the Pinscher, the Rottweiler, the Manchester Terrier and, possibly, the Pointer.

COAT Smooth, short, thick and close.
COLOUR Solid black, brown, blue or fawn with rust markings .
FEATURES Almond-shaped eyes; small, neat ears set high on head; well-arched neck; square body; tail characteristically docked at second joint.
SIZE Height at withers: dogs 65–70cm (25$\frac{1}{2}$–27$\frac{1}{2}$in), bitches 60–65cm (25$\frac{1}{2}$–26in). Weight: 30–40kg (66–88lb).
CARE Needs knowledgeable handling and training and lots of exercise.
CHARACTER An alert, aloof guard dog. Loyal and devoted to owner.

GERMAN SHEPHERD DOG

This popular breed is said to be descended from Bronze Age wolves. The breed we know today was first shown in Hanover in 1882.

COAT Medium length, straight, hard and close-lying, with a thick undercoat.
COLOUR Solid black or grey; black saddle with tan or gold to light grey markings; grey with lighter or brown markings.
FEATURES Medium-sized eyes and ears; long neck; long shoulder blades; straight back; strong hindquarters, broad and well muscled; long, bushy tail.
SIZE Height at top of shoulders: dogs 60–65cm (24–25$\frac{1}{2}$in), bitches 55–60cm (22–24in). Weight 34–43kg (75–95lb).
CARE Needs vigorous daily grooming and plenty of exercise.
CHARACTER Intelligent, strong and agile. A great worker, obedience or agility dog.

GREAT DANE

Said to be descended from the Molossus dog, the Great Dane was used for wild-boar hunting in the Middle Ages.

COAT Short, dense and sleek.
COLOUR Brindle, fawn, blue, black or harlequin.
FEATURES Large, wide and open nostrils; fairly deep-set eyes; triangular ears; very deep body; long tail, thick at the root and tapering towards the tip.
SIZE Minimum height over 18 months: dogs 76cm (30in), bitches 71cm (28in). Minimum weight over 18 months: dogs 55kg (120lb), bitches 45kg (100lb).
CARE Should be kept indoors. Needs regular exercise on hard ground and daily grooming with a body brush.
CHARACTER Good-natured, playful and easy to train.

ROTTWEILER

An ancient breed used as a wild-boar hunter, cattle dog and, more recently, as a police dog and guard.

COAT Medium length, coarse and lying flat, with undercoat on neck and thighs.
COLOUR Black with clearly defined tan or deep brown markings.
FEATURES Head broad between the ears; almond-shaped eyes; small ears; powerful, neck; broad, deep chest; tail docked at first joint and usually carried horizontally.
SIZE Height at shoulders: dogs 60–68cm (24–27in), bitches 55–64cm (22–25in). Weight: 41–50kg (90–110lb).
CARE Requires kindly but firm handling, plenty of space and exercise, and daily grooming with a bristle brush.
CHARACTER A courageous, loyal dog that makes an excellent companion-guard.

HUNGARIAN PULI

The Puli is said to be descended from sheepdogs brought over to Hungary by the Magyars 1,000 years ago.

COAT Dense and weatherproof; outer coat wavy or curly, undercoat soft, woolly.
COLOUR Black, rusty black, white or various shades of grey and apricot.
FEATURES Small, fine head with domed skull; ears set slightly below top of skull; withers slightly higher than level of back; medium-length tail curls over loins.
SIZE Height at withers: dogs 40–44cm (16–17½in), bitches 37–40cm (14½–16in). Weight: dogs 13–15kg (28½–33lb), bitches 10–13kg (22–28½lb).
CARE Cords of the coat have to be separated by hand, brushed and combed.
CHARACTER A devoted, obedient and intelligent dog. Can be shy with strangers.

SIBERIAN HUSKY

A dog of great beauty, strength and stamina, the Siberian Husky has the Chukchi Sled Dog as an ancestor.

COAT Medium in length.
COLOUR All colours and markings allowed in show dogs.
FEATURES Medium-sized head in proportion to body; almond-shaped eyes; medium-sized ears; arched neck; strong body with a straight back; well-furred tail carried gracefully curled over back except when resting.
SIZE Height: 53–60cm (21–23½in). Weight: 16–27kg (35–60lb).
CARE Can be kept as a family pet, but needs some work and plenty of space and exercise.
CHARACTER Intelligent, friendly and reliable; easy to train.

SAMOYED

Brought to Britain from Siberia in 1889, the Samoyed, or "Smiling Sammy", is a beautiful spitz variety that has great powers of endurance and was used on Arctic expeditions.

COAT Harsh, but not wiry, and straight, with thick, soft, short undercoat.
COLOUR Pure white, white and biscuit, cream; outer coat silver-tipped.
FEATURES Broad head; dark, almond-shaped eyes; thick ears, not too large, and slightly rounded at the tips; medium length back; long, profusely coated tail that is carried curled over the back.
SIZE Height at withers: dogs 53–59cm (21–23½in), bitches 48–53cm (19–21in). Weight: 23–30kg (50–65lb).
CARE The thick, water-resistant coat needs regular brushing and combing.
CHARACTER A devoted dog, good with children, that makes an obedient pet.

AMERICAN COCKER SPANIEL

One of the top breeds in the US, the American Cocker Spaniel was bred from one English-bred bitch brought over from Britain in the 1880s.

COAT Short and fine on head, medium length on body, with enough undercoat to give protection.

COLOUR Black, jet black; black and tan and brown and tan, with definite tan markings on jet black or brown body; particolours and tricolours. Check with breed standard for full requirements.

FEATURES Head rounded and well-developed; eyes full and looking directly forwards; back slopes slightly downwards from shoulders to tail; tail characteristically docked.

SIZE Height: dogs 35–38cm (14–15in), bitches 33–35cm (13–14in). Weight: 11–13kg (24–28lb).

CARE Pets need daily brushing and combing. Show dogs need to be trimmed with clippers and scissors.

CHARACTER A useful, all-purpose gundog. A popular show dog and fine pet.

CLUMBER SPANIEL

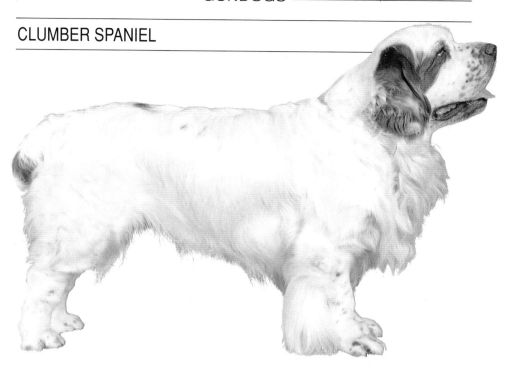

The Clumber is the heaviest of the spaniels, with the Basset and the now extinct Alpine Spaniel in its ancestry. A favourite of several generations of the British royal family, the Clumber is slower than lighter-boned dogs in the field, but is nevertheless a good, steady gundog, excelling in flushing out game over rough ground and as a retriever.

COAT Abundant, close and silky.
COLOUR Plain white body with lemon markings preferred for show dogs, though orange is allowed. Slight head markings and freckled muzzle.
FEATURES Massive, square, medium-length head; clean, dark-amber eyes, slightly sunken; large, vine-leaf shaped ears; long, heavy body close to ground; chest deep; tail set low and feathered.
SIZE Height at withers: dogs 48–51cm (19–20in), bitches 43–48cm (17–19in). Weight: dogs 32–38kg (70–84lb), bitches 25–32kg (55–70lb).
CARE Needs a fair amount of brushing and care must be taken that mud does not become lodged between its toes.
CHARACTER Good temperament and may be kept as a pet, but ideally it should be a working gundog.

FIELD SPANIEL

The British Field Spaniel is, in effect, a larger version of the Cocker Spaniel.

COAT Long, flat and glossy, without curls; silky in texture.
COLOUR Black, liver or roan with tan markings; clear black, white or liver and white unacceptable in show dogs.
FEATURES Head conveys impression of high breeding; eyes wide open; moderately long, wide ears; deep chest; tail set low and usually docked.
SIZE Height at withers: dogs about 46cm (18in), bitches about 43cm (17in). Weight: 16–25kg (35–55lb).
CARE Needs plenty of exercise and daily brush and comb so the coat does not become matted.
CHARACTER Responsible and friendly.

SUSSEX SPANIEL

One of the rarer spaniels, the Sussex spaniel has been known in southern England for around 200 years.

COAT Abundant and flat; ample, weather-resistant undercoat.
COLOUR Rich golden liver, shading to golden at tips of hairs; dark liver or puce is undesirable in show dogs.
FEATURES Wide head, slightly rounded between the ears; hazel eyes with a soft expression; fairly large, thick ears; deep, well-developed chest; tail set on low and never carried above level of back.
SIZE Height at withers: 33–40cm (13–16in). Weight: 16–23kg (35–50lb).
CARE Requires a daily brush and comb.
CHARACTER A working spaniel with an excellent nose that will "give tongue", or bay, when it has found game. Loyal and easy to train.

ENGLISH SPRINGER SPANIEL

The English Springer is one of the oldest of the British spaniels, with the exception of the Clumber. It is the ancestor of most other contemporary spaniels. Spaniels were originally used to flush out, or "spring", game from cover.

COAT Close, straight and weather-resistant; never coarse.
COLOUR Liver and white, black and white, either of these with tan markings.
FEATURES Medium-length skull; medium-sized eyes; long, wide ears; strong body; tail set low, and never carried above the level of the back.
SIZE Height at shoulders: dogs 51cm (20in), bitches 48cm (19in). Weight: 22–25kg (49–55lb).
CARE Needs plenty of exercise, a daily brushing and checks to ensure that mud does not become lodged in its paws.
CHARACTER Intelligent, loyal. Makes a good gundog and family pet.

WELSH SPRINGER SPANIEL

The Welsh Springer Spaniel, or its forerunner, are mentioned in the Laws of Wales, which date back to AD1300. It is possible that this red and white spaniel is a cross between the English Springer and the Clumber.

COAT Straight and flat, silky in texture; some feathering on chest, underside of body and legs.
COLOUR Rich red and white.
FEATURES Slightly domed head; medium-sized, hazel or dark eyes; ears set moderately low; strong muscular body; tail well set on and low.
SIZE Height at withers: dogs 45–48cm (18–19in), bitches 43–45cm (17–18in). Weight: 16–20kg (35–45lb).
CARE Needs daily brushing and checks for mud lodged in paws and ears.
CHARACTER Loyal, hardworking and friendly. Has an excellent nose and is a good swimmmer.

FLAT-COATED RETRIEVER

This British breed is thought to have evolved from the Labrador Retriever and spaniels.

COAT Dense, fine to medium texture and medium length.
COLOUR Solid black or solid liver.
FEATURES Long, clean head; medium-sized eyes; small ears well set on; deep chest and strong body; tail short, straight and well set on.
SIZE Height: dogs 58–61cm (23–24in), bitches 56–58cm (22–23in). Weight: dogs about 27–36kg (60–80lb), bitches 25–32kg (55–70lb).
CARE Can be kept outside. Needs plenty of exercise and daily brushing.
CHARACTER Intelligent, loyal, affectionate.

LABRADOR RETRIEVER

The breed arrived in Britain in the 1830s from Newfoundland, where it was used to help fishermen land their nets. Today, it is a family pet, a gundog, an obedience dog, a show dog and works as a guide dog for the blind.

COAT Short and dense, without wave or feathering; weather-resistant undercoat.
COLOUR Black, yellow or liver/chocolate; yellows range from cream to red fox.
FEATURES Head broad with defined stop; medium-sized eyes; ears not large or heavy; chest of good width and depth; distinctive "otter" tail.

SIZE Height at shoulders: 56–61cm (22–24in). Weight: dogs 27–34kg (60–75lb), bitches 25–32kg (55–70b).
CARE Needs plenty of exercise, to avoid obesity, and regular brushing.
CHARACTER Exuberant when young, but easy to train. Responsive, friendly.

GOLDEN RETRIEVER

This breed is thought to be the result of a retriever-spaniel cross. There is a story that their true ancestors were a troupe of performing Russian shepherd dogs.

COAT Flat or wavy with good feathering; dense, water-resistant undercoat.
COLOUR Any shade of gold or cream.
FEATURES Balanced and well-chiselled head; dark brown eyes; moderate-sized ears; deep chest and well-balanced body; tail set on and carried level with back.
SIZE Height at withers: dogs 56–61cm (22–24in), bitches 51–56cm (20–22in). Weight: 25–34kg (55–75lb),
CARE Needs regular brushing and ample exercise.
CHARACTER Excellent gundog, of kindly temperament and gentle with children.

IRISH SETTER

The Irish Setter, or Red Setter, was developed by crossing Irish Water Spaniels, Spanish Pointers and the English and Gordon Setters. Although it originated in Ireland, the breed came into its own in Victorian England, where its speed and energy made it ideal as a gundog working in large open expanses of countryside.

COAT Short and fine on head, fronts of legs and tips of ears; moderately long, free and as straight as possible on rest of body; good feathering.

COLOUR Rich chestnut with no trace of black; white markings on chest, throat, chin or toes, or small star on forehead or narrow streak or blaze on nose or face are allowed when showing.

FEATURES Long, lean head; dark hazel to dark brown eyes; moderate-sized ears; deep chest, rather narrow in front; tail moderate in length in relation to body.

SIZE Height: 64–68cm (25–27in). Weight: 27–32kg (60–70lb).

CARE Requires plenty of exercise and daily brushing.

CHARACTER Very good-natured and loving with boundless energy. But does not make a good guard dog.

IRISH WATER SPANIEL

Evidence for water dogs and water spaniels goes back to AD17 and some form of water spaniel has been known in Ireland for more than 1,000 years. The Irish Water Spaniel, the tallest of the spaniels, is thought to have been developed through crosses with Poodles and Curly-coated Retrievers. Before 1859 there were two separate strains of the breed in Ireland, one in the north and one in the south. It would seem that the southern strain, which resembled the Standard Poodle, formed the basis of the modern breed.

COAT Dense, tight ringlets on neck, body and top part of tail; longer, curling hair on legs and topknot; face, rear of tail and back of legs below hocks smooth.
COLOUR Rich, dark liver.
FEATURES Good-sized, high-domed head; small, almond-shaped eyes; long, oval-shaped ears; long, arching neck; deep chest; short tail.
SIZE Height: dogs 53–60cm (21–24in), bitches 51–58cm (20–23in). Weight: dogs 25–30kg (55–66lb), bitches 20.5–26kg (45–58lb).
CARE Needs to be groomed at least once a week with a steel comb. Some stripping and trimming round feet is necessary.
CHARACTER Brave, loving and intelligent. Has a fine nose and will work and quarter as a spaniel. A strong swimmer that is large enough to retrieve large game, such as geese, from deep water.

ENGLISH SETTER

GORDON SETTER

The English Setter is the oldest and most distinctive of the setter breeds, which sit or "set" when they find prey.

COAT Short, straight and dense.
COLOUR Black and white (blue belton), orange and white (orange belton), lemon and white (lemon belton), liver and white (liver belton), or tricolour (blue belton and tan, or liver belton and tan).
FEATURES Head, lean and noble; ears moderately low set; back short, level and well-muscled; high withers; tail set in line with back, well-feathered.
SIZE Height: dogs 62–68cm (24½–27in), bitches 60–62cm (24½–25in). Weight: 18–32kg (40–71lb).
CARE Needs only daily brushing with a stiff brush and steel comb, requires a great deal of exercise.
CHARACTER Loyal and affectionate.

The Gordon is the only Scottish gundog. It was bred in the 1770s by the 4th Duke of Richmond and Gordon from blood-hounds and collies, among others.

COAT Short and fine on head, fronts of legs and tips of ears; moderately long over rest of body, flat and free from curl.
COLOUR Deep, shining coal black without rustiness, and with lustrous tan markings.
FEATURES Head deep rather than broad; dark brown eyes; medium-sized ears; tail straight or slightly curved, not too long.
SIZE Height at shoulders: dogs 60–70cm (24–27½in), bitches 57–65cm (22½–25½in). Weight: dogs 25–36kg (55–80lb), bitches 20–32kg (45–71lb).
CARE Needs plenty of space and lots of exercise. Coat needs daily brushing.
CHARACTER Easy-going, calm and docile. A methodical, tireless hunter.

POINTER

The Pointer is famed for its stance, pointing with its nose and tail in the direction of game. Pointing dogs first appeared in Europe in the 17th century.

COAT Short, dense and smooth.
COLOUR Lemon and white, orange and white, liver and white, black and white; self (pure) colours and tricolours.
FEATURES Medium-width head with pronounced stop; dark, round eyes; ears on level with eyes; thin, sloping shoulders; deep chest; tail tapering to a point.
SIZE Height at withers: dogs 64–70cm (25–27$\frac{1}{2}$in), bitches 58–66cm (23–26in). Weight: dogs 25–34kg (55–75lb), bitches 20–30kg (45–65lb).
CARE Needs regular brushing and plenty of exercise.
CHARACTER Affectionate, obedient, easy to train and good with children.

WEIMARANER

The Weimaraner, or "Silver Ghost", is said to have been bred in the 19th century by the Grand Duke of Weimar.

COAT Short, smooth and sleek.
COLOUR Silver grey is preferred for showing, but shades of mouse or roe grey are allowed.
FEATURES Head moderately long and aristocratic; medium-sized eyes; long ears; deep chest and moderately long body; tail characteristically docked.
SIZE Height at withers: dogs 60–70cm (24–27$\frac{1}{2}$in), bitches 56–64cm (22–25in). Weight: 32–38kg (70–84lb).
CARE Best housed indoors, rather than in a kennel, and requires little grooming.
CHARACTER Good-natured and intelligent.

GERMAN POINTER

The German Short-haired Pointer is of Spanish origin and was probably derived from crossing the Spanish Pointer with a scenthound, thereby producing a dog that would both point and trail. English Foxhound blood is also believed to have been added. The breed was developed in Germany about 100 years ago.

COAT Short-haired: short and flat, coarse to the touch. Wire-haired: thick and harsh, with dense undercoat.

COLOUR Short-haired: solid liver, liver and white spotted, liver and white spotted and ticked; liver and white ticked; the same variations with black instead of liver; not tricoloured. Wire-haired: liver and white, solid liver, also black and white; solid black and tricolour undesirable in show dogs.

FEATURES Short-haired: broad, clean-cut head, with slightly moulded crown; medium-sized eyes; broad ears set on high; chest should appear deep rather than wide, but in proportion to body; tail starts high and thick, growing gradually thinner towards tip. Wire-haired: broad head balanced in proportion to body; slightly rounded crown; medium-sized, oval eyes; ears medium-sized in relation to head; chest should appear deep rather than wide but not out of proportion to rest of body; tail starts high and thick, growing gradually thinner towards tip.

SIZE Short-haired – height at withers: dogs 58–64cm (23–25in), bitches 53–58cm (21–23in). Weight: dogs

Except for its bristly coat, the German Wire-haired Pointer (right) is very similar to the Short-haired, which contributed to its make-up.

25–32kg (55–71lb), bitches 20–27kg (44–60lb). Wire-haired – height at shoulders: dogs 60–63cm (24–25in), bitches 56–61cm (22–24in). Weight: dogs 25–34kg (55–75lb), bitches 20–29kg (44–64lb).

CARE Neither breed requires a lot of grooming. Wire-haired is less suitable as a household pet. Both types need plenty of exercise.

CHARACTER Short-haired is easy to train and good with children. Wire-haired Pointer is an active, responsive dog, but it has some aggressive qualities.

HUNGARIAN VIZSLA

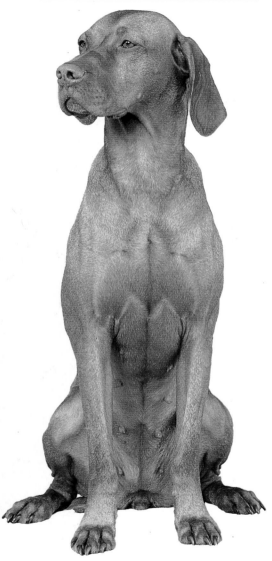

The Hungarian Vizsla, or Magyar Vizsla, is the national hunting dog of Hungary. The Hungarian word *vizsla* means "responsive" or "alert". This smooth-haired setter was bred for the temperature extremes of the central Hungarian plain (Puszta). It is likely that the German Weimaraner, to which it bears a strong resemblance, and Transylvanian pointing dogs played a part in its early development. There is a wire-haired form of the Vizsla, rarer than the smooth-haired variety, which is favoured in its native Hungary for working in water. It was not until after the Second World War that the Vizsla became widely known.

COAT Short, dense and straight; tightly fitting.

COLOUR Russet gold; in show dogs, small white marks on chest and feet are acceptable.

FEATURES Lean, elegant head with a long muzzle; long, thin ears, set moderately low; short, level, well-muscled back; deep chest with prominent breastbone; tail moderately thick, set low and docked.

SIZE Height at withers: dogs 57–64cm (22 1/2 –25in), bitches 53–60cm (21–24in). Weight: 20–30kg (44–66lb).

CARE Needs plenty of exercise and the coat should be brushed regularly.

CHARACTER A versatile, easily trained gundog adept at hunting, pointing and retrieving. It is gentle and responsive, is good with children and makes a first-class pet.

ITALIAN SPINONE

The Italian Spinone is an ancient gundog breed. It has also recently become a contender in the international show ring and in field trials. Opinions about the dog's origins vary, as to whether it is of setter descent, a relative of the coarse-haired Italian Segugio or a Griffon cross. Yet others believe this powerful, versatile hunter originated in France, later finding its way to Piedmont in Italy, and that its evolution is attributable to the French Griffon, German Pointers, the Porcelaine, the Barbet and the Korthals Griffon. The Spinone may be the result of a mating between a Coarse-haired Setter and a white Mastiff.

COAT Rough, thick, fairly wiry with a dense undercoat.
COLOUR White, white with orange markings, solid white peppered orange, white with brown markings, white speckled with brown (brown roan), with or without brown markings.
FEATURES Expressive eyes, varying in colour from yellow to ochre; long, triangular ears; sturdy back; body length equal to height at withers; tail thick at base, carried horizontally.
SIZE Height at shoulders: dogs 59–69cm (23–27in), bitches 58–64cm (23–25in). Weight: dogs 32–37kg (70–82lb), bitches 28–32kg (62–70lb).
CARE Needs plenty of vigorous exercise, is a fine swimmer and is best suited to country life.
CHARACTER Affectionate, agreeable and loyal. Will point and has a soft mouth for retrieving game undamaged.

OTTERHOUND

The strongly built British Otterhound probably evolved from foxhounds and other hunting dogs.

COAT Long, about 5cm (2in), dense, rough and harsh, but not wiry.
COLOUR All hound colours.
FEATURES Clean, very imposing head; intelligent eyes; long, pendulous ears – a unique feature of the breed – set on level with corner of eyes; deep chest with fairly deep, well-sprung rib-cage; tail (stern) set on high, carried up when alert or moving.

SIZE Height: dogs 60–68cm (24–27in), bitches 58–66cm (23–26in). Weight: dogs 34–52kg (75–115lb), bitches 30–45kg (66–100lb).
CARE Can be kennelled outdoors. Needs a lot of exercise and its rough coat should be groomed once a week and bathed as necessary.
CHARACTER Amiable, but stubborn. Can be destructive if undisciplined.

BEAGLE

The Beagle has existed in the UK at least since the reign of King Henry VIII (1491–1547). Sometimes known as the "singing Beagle", this breed is not noisy indoors, reserving its voice for the chase.

COAT Short, dense and weatherproof.
COLOUR Any recognized hound colour other than liver; tip of stern, white.
FEATURES Head fairly long and powerful without being coarse; dark brown or hazel eyes; long ears with pointed tips; top-line straight and level; moderately long, sturdy tail.
SIZE Height: two US varieties – under 33cm (13in) and 33–37.5cm (13–15in); UK – height at withers 33–40cm (13–16in). Weight: 8–13.5kg (18–30lb).
CARE Coat needs little or no attention; pet dogs need only average exercise.
CHARACTER Affectionate and determined.

WHIPPET

The Whippet, which originated in 19th-century Britain, is the fastest breed in the world, reaching speeds of almost 60km/h (37mph).

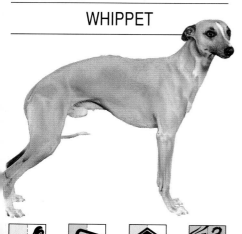

COAT Short, fine and close.
COLOUR Any colour or mixture of colours.
FEATURES Long, lean head, bright, oval-shaped eyes with a very alert expression; rose-shaped ears; very deep chest with plenty of heart room; long, tapering tail with no feathering.
SIZE Height: dogs 47–51cm (18½–20in), bitches 44–47cm (17½–18½in). Weight: about 12.5kg (28lb).
CARE Should be housed indoors; needs plenty of exercise; coat needs only a brush and rub-down.
CHARACTER Gentle and affectionate.

IRISH WOLFHOUND

Over 2,000 years old, the Irish Wolfhound – the tallest dog in the world – is a very popular breed.

COAT Rough, harsh.
COLOUR Grey, steel grey, brindle, red, black, pure white, fawn or wheaten.
FEATURES Long, strong head carried high; dark eyes; small, rose-shaped ears; very deep chest; long, slightly curved tail.
SIZE Minimum height: dogs 80cm (31in), bitches 75cm (30in); optimum height: 80–85cm (31–33½in). Minimum weight: dogs 55kg (121lb), bitches 48kg (106lb).
CARE Needs only average exercise; can be kept indoors.
CHARACTER Gentle, calm and friendly.

BASSET HOUND

This breed was developed in Britain in the 1800s for hunting in thick cover.

COAT Hard, smooth, short and dense.
COLOUR Generally black, white and tan or lemon and white.
FEATURES Head domed, with some stop; lozenge-shaped eyes; ears set low; body long and deep; tail (stern) well set on.
SIZE Height at withers: 33–35cm (13–14in). Weight: 18–27kg (40–60lb).
CARE Fencing is essential as Bassets tend to wander.
CHARACTER Energetic, independent.

BLOODHOUND

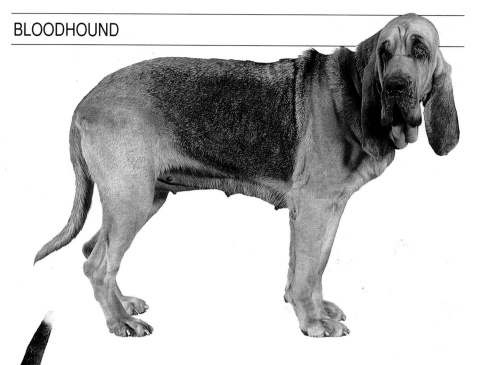

The Bloodhound, also called the Chien de Saint Hubert, is one of the oldest hound breeds. It originated in France in the 9th century, but its ancestors are thought to have been bred in Mesopotamia in 2,000–1,000BC. Bloodhounds have the keenest sense of smell of any domestic animal and have been used to track down lost people as well for hunting game.

COAT Smooth, short and weatherproof.
COLOUR Black and tan, liver and tan, red.
FEATURES Head narrow in proportion to length, and long in proportion to body; medium-sized eyes; thin, soft ears set very low; well-sprung ribs; tail (stern) long, thick and tapering to a point.
SIZE Height: dogs 64–68 (25–27)cm, bitches 58–64 in (23–25in).
Weight: dogs 41–50kg (90–110lb), bitches 36–45kg (80–100lb).
CARE An active dog that needs a great deal of exercise. Should be groomed daily with a hound glove.
CHARACTER Determined, affectionate and lively. Has a distinctive bay (call).

DACHSHUND

Long-haired
Dachshund (left).

There are six varieties of Dachshund,
which is also known as the Teckel or
Badger Hound. They are the Smooth-
haired, the Long-haired and the Wire-
haired. Each variety occurs as both a
Standard and Miniature. The Dachshund
derives from the oldest breeds of
German hunting dogs, such as the
Bibarhund, and is known to have existed
as long ago as the 16th century.
Originally there was only one variety, the
Smooth-haired Dachshund, whose
wrinkled paws are a characteristic now
rarely seen. The Wire-haired was
produced through the introduction of
Dandie Dinmont and other terrier blood,
while the Long-haired was formed by
introducing the German Stöber, a
gundog, to a Smooth-haired Dachshund
and Spaniel cross.

Wire-haired
Dachshund.

COAT Smooth-haired: dense, short and smooth. Long-haired: soft and straight, and only slightly wavy. Wire-haired: short, straight and harsh, with a long undercoat.

COLOUR All colours but white permissible when showing; small patch on chest permitted but not desirable; dappled dogs may include white but should be evenly marked all over.

FEATURES Long head, conical in appearance when seen from above; medium-sized eyes; ears set high; body long and full-muscled; tail continues along line of spine but is slightly curved.

SIZE Height: 13–23cm (5–9in). Weight: Standard – USA 7–15kg (15–33lb), UK 9–12kg (20–26lb); Miniature – USA under 5kg (11lb), UK about 4.5kg (10lb).

CARE Short-haired needs only daily grooming with a hound glove and soft cloth. Wire-haired and Long-haired should be brushed and combed. Dachshunds are prone to back problems and should not jump on or from heights.

CHARACTER Active and devoted. Makes a good family pet and watchdog – it has a loud bark for its size.

Smooth-haired
Dachshund.

BORZOI

The Borzoi, or Russian Wolfhound, was used in imperial Russia from the 17th century for wolf coursing – the Borzoi tracked the wolf, when it was beaten from cover, but did not kill it. The dog's task was to grab the wolf by the neck and throw it, whereupon it would be killed with a blow from a dagger. Originally there were various strains of Borzoi, including the Sudanese Borzoi, but the strain developed in Russia forms the basis for today's breed standard. The name comes from the Russian word, *borzii*, for swift.

COAT Silky, flat and wavy or rather curly; never woolly.

COLOUR Any colour acceptable.
FEATURES Long, lean head, in proportion to overall size; dark eyes with intelligent, alert expression; small, pointed ears; chest deep and narrow; long tail.
SIZE Minimum height at withers: dogs 74cm (29in), bitches 68cm (27in). Weight: dogs 34–48kg (75–105lb), bitches about 7–9kg (15–20lb) less.
CARE Should be kept away from livestock; coat needs little attention.
CHARACTER Elegant, intelligent and faithful, but a little aloof.

SALUKI

The Saluki, which dates back to 3,000BC, may take its name from the ancient city of Saluk in the Yemen, or from the town of Seleukia in the ancient Hellenic empire in Syria. It is prized by the Bedouin people for hunting gazelle, but elsewhere in the world it is kept as a companion and show dog. It is also known as the Gazelle Hound, the Arab Gazelle Hound, the Eastern Greyhound and the Persian Greyhound.

COAT Smooth, silky in texture.
COLOUR White, cream, fawn, golden, red, grizzle, silver grizzle, deer grizzle, tricolour (white, black and tan) and variations of these colours.

FEATURES Long, narrow head; eyes dark to hazel; long, mobile ears, not set too low; fairly broad back; strong hip bones set wide apart; tail set on from long, gently sloping pelvis.
SIZE Height: 56–71cm (22–28in). Weight: 20–30kg (44–66lb).
CARE Requires plenty of exercise; coat needs daily grooming using a brush and hound glove.
CHARACTER Loyal, affectionate and trustworthy; its hunting instincts needs to be controlled around livestock.

AFGHAN HOUND

GREYHOUND

The Afghan Hound is an ancient breed, said to have been one of the animals aboard Noah's Ark! A member of the Greyhound family, its ancestors found their way to Afghanistan from Persia (Iran) where the breed developed its thick coat to withstand the harsh climate.

COAT Long and fine.
COLOUR All colours acceptable.
FEATURES Head long and not too narrow; eyes preferably dark, but golden not debarred; ears set low and well back; moderate-length, level back; tail not too short.
SIZE Height: dogs 68cm (27in), bitches 63cm (25in). Weight: dogs 27kg (60lb), bitches 23kg (50lb).
CARE Coat needs regular attention.
CHARACTER Intelligent and aloof but affectionate; generally good-natured.

The Greyhound is possibly the purest breed on Earth, having changed little from dogs depicted on the tombs of Egyptian pharaohs. It is thought the Celts brought the Greyhound to Britain.

COAT Fine and close.
COLOUR Black, white, red, blue, fawn, fallow brindle, or any of these colours broken with white.
FEATURES Long, moderately broad head; bright, intelligent eyes; small, close-shaped ears; long, elegant neck; deep, chest; long tail set on rather low.
SIZE Height: dogs 71–76cm (28–30in), bitches 68–71cm (27–28in). Weight: dogs about 30–32kg (66–70lb), bitches about 27–30kg (60–66lb).
CARE Needs a daily brush and average but regular exercise on hard ground.
CHARACTER Gentle and faithful.

RHODESIAN RIDGEBACK

Named after Rhodesia, now Zimbabwe, in southern Africa, this breed has a ridge of hair growing in the reverse direction down the middle of its back. It is also known as the Lion Dog because packs of them were used to hunt lions.

COAT Short, dense, sleek and glossy.
COLOUR Light wheaten to red wheaten.
FEATURES Flat skull, broad between ears; round eyes, set moderately well apart; ears set rather high; chest very deep but not too wide; tail strong at root and tapering towards tip.
SIZE Height at withers: dogs 64–67cm (25–26½in), bitches 61–66cm (24–26in). Weight: 30–34kg (66–75lb).
CARE Needs plenty of exercise and daily grooming with a hound glove.
CHARACTER Obedient, good with children and will guard its owners with its life.

BASENJI

The Basenji, which means "bush thing", comes from central Africa. It is famous for being the only dog without a bark.

COAT Short, sleek, close and very fine.
COLOUR Black, red, or black and tan; all should have white on chest, on feet and tail tips; white blaze, collar and legs optional; black and tan with tan melon pips and black, tan and white mask.
FEATURES Dark, almond-shaped eyes; small, pointed ears; well-balanced body with short, level back; tail set on high, curling tightly over spine and lying close to thigh, with a single or double curve.
SIZE Height: 40–43cm (16–17in). Weight: 9.5–11kg (21–24lb).
CARE Needs only a daily rub-down.
CHARACTER Playful, loving and intelligent.

BULL TERRIER

STAFFORDSHIRE BULL TERRIER

The Bull Terrier began life as a cross between an Old English Bulldog and a terrier, and was originally a fighting dog.

COAT Short and flat.
COLOUR Pure white, brindled, or black, red and fawn tricolour
FEATURES Long straight head, deep right to end of muzzle; eyes appear narrow; small, thin ears set close together; short tail, set on low and carried horizontally.
SIZE Height: 53–56cm (21–22in). Weight: 23.5–28kg (52–62lb).
CARE Needs careful training and an able-bodied owner. Its short, flat coat is easy to look after.
CHARACTER Despite its fierce appearance and strength, it makes a faithful and devoted pet. The bitch, in particular, is very reliable with children.

Derived from crossing an Old English Bulldog and a terrier when dog fighting was a "sport" in Britain.

COAT Smooth, short and dense.
COLOUR Red, fawn, white, black or blue, or any of these with white. Any shade of brindle or brindle with white.
FEATURES Short, broad skull; rose or half-pricked ears; eyes preferably dark; close-coupled body; medium-length tail.
SIZE Height: 36–41cm (14–16in). Weight: 11–17kg (24–37lb).
CARE Easy to look after, only needing regular brushing.
CHARACTER Affectionate, fun companion.

AIREDALE TERRIER

The Airedale is the largest member of the terrier group. It was created by crossing a working terrier with an Otterhound. It is an expert rat- and duck-catcher and can be trained to the gun.

COAT Hard, dense and wiry.
COLOUR Body-saddle, top of neck and top of tail, black or grizzle; all other parts tan.
FEATURES Long, flat skull; small, dark eyes; V-shaped ears; deep chest; short, strong, level back; tail set on high, customarily docked.
SIZE Height: dogs 58–61cm (23–24in), bitches 56–58cm (22–23in) Weight: about 20kg (44lb).
CARE Requires plenty of exercise. If you want to exhibit, needs to be hand-stripped twice a year.
CHARACTER Extremely loyal, good with children and an excellent guard dog.

BEDLINGTON TERRIER

Once a favourite for accompanying poachers, it's believed the Greyhound or Whippet played a part in the Bedlington Terrier's ancestry.

COAT Thick and linty.
COLOUR Blue, liver or sandy, with or without tan.
FEATURES Narrow skull; small, bright, deep-set eyes; moderate-sized, filbert-shaped ears; muscular body; moderate-length tail, tapering to a point.
SIZE Height at withers: dogs 40–44cm (16–17½in), bitches 38–40cm (15–16in). Weight: 8–10.5kg (17½–23lb).
CARE Coat needs regular trimming and a daily grooming.
CHARACTER Lovable, full of fun, easily trained.

FOX TERRIER

Smooth-haired

The Smooth Fox Terrier started life as a stable dog, its job being to hunt vermin. It probably descends from terriers in the English counties of Cheshire and Shropshire, with some Beagle blood added. The Wire, which is a great rabbiter, originated in the coal-mining areas of Durham and Derbyshire in England, and in Wales. As their names imply, they will also pursue foxes.

For many years, the Smooth and Wire Fox Terriers were bred together, regardless of coat. All the great Wires resulted from the mating of a Smooth Fox Terrier called Jock with a bitch of unknown antecedents, but definitely wire-haired, called Trap. The Smooth was given its own register in 1876, three years after the British Kennel Club was founded, but the conformation of the two breeds remains the same. The Wire is more popular than its smooth-coated relative, which is rarely seen outside the show ring.

Wire-haired

COAT Smooth: straight, flat and smooth. Wire: dense and very wiry.

COLOUR Smooth: all white; white with tan or black markings – white should predominate; brindle, red or liver markings highly undesirable. Wire: white should predominate with black or tan markings; brindle, red, liver or slate-blue markings undesirable.

FEATURES Smooth: flat, moderately narrow skull; dark, small eyes, rather deep set; small, V-shaped ears dropping forward close to cheek; chest deep, not broad; tail customarily docked. Wire: top line of skull almost flat; dark, bright eyes; small V-shaped ears of moderate thickness; short, strong, level back; tail customarily docked.

SIZE Maximum height at withers: dogs 39cm (15½in), bitches slightly less. Weight: 7–8kg (15½–17½lb).

CARE The Smooth needs daily grooming with a stiff brush, and trimming and chalking before a show. The Wire needs to be hand-stripped three times a year, and to be groomed regularly.

CHARACTER Affectionate and trainable, and an ideal small child's companion.

LAKELAND TERRIER

Originating from Cumberland in England, the Lakeland Terrier was developed, from various terrier crossings, to protect lambs.

COAT Dense and harsh, with weather-resistant undercoat.

COLOUR Black and tan, blue and tan, red, wheaten, red grizzle, liver, blue or black.

FEATURES Flat skull; refined, dark or hazel eyes; reasonably narrow chest; tail customarily docked.

SIZE Maximum height at shoulders: 37cm (14$\frac{1}{2}$in). Weight: dogs about 8kg (17$\frac{1}{2}$lb), bitches about 7kg (15$\frac{1}{2}$lb).

CARE Coat requires daily brushing and, if to be exhibited, needs to be stripped three times a year.

CHARACTER Brave, intelligent and hardy; makes a good housepet or guard dog.

MANCHESTER TERRIER

The Manchester Terrier's ancestors were sporting terriers that would kill rats in a pit for the amusement of spectators in the mid 19th century. It is related to the Whippet and the Dachshund.

COAT Close, smooth, short and glossy.

COLOUR Jet black and rich tan.

FEATURES Long, flat, narrow skull; small, dark, sparkling eyes; small, V-shaped ears; chest narrow and deep; short tail, set on where arch of back ends.

SIZE Height at shoulders: dogs about 40cm (16in), bitches 38cm (15in). Weight: 5.5–10kg (12–22lb).

CARE The only grooming required is a daily brush and rub-down.

CHARACTER Lively, devoted, and long-lived; makes a good pet despite its sporting past.

GLEN OF IMAAL TERRIER

This short-legged terrier comes from County Wicklow, Ireland. Originally used to get rid of vermin, it is now found mainly as a family pet or as a working terrier on Irish farms.

COAT Medium length and harsh textured, with a soft undercoat.
COLOUR Blue, brindle or wheaten.
FEATURES Wide, longish head with a strong foreface; brown eyes; small ears, pricked when alert; powerful jaws; deep, medium-length body; tail strong at root, well set on, docking optional.
SIZE Height: about 35cm (14in). Weight: about 16kg (35lb).
CARE Maintaining its "shaggy-dog" look requires only a daily brushing.
CHARACTER Affectionate, brave, playful.

IRISH TERRIER

Some claim the Irish Terrier is a smaller version of the Irish Wolfhound, but it seems more likely it is a descendant of Black and Tan Terriers.

COAT Harsh and wiry.
COLOUR Whole-coloured, preferably red, red wheaten or yellow-red.
FEATURES Long head, flat and narrow between ears; small, dark eyes; small V-shaped ears; deep, muscular tail.
SIZE Height at shoulders: about 46cm (18in). Weight: 11.5–12kg (25–26½lb).
CARE Its coat should be stripped two or three times a year, and it should be groomed regularly.
CHARACTER Can be trained to the gun and makes an affectionate pet.

BORDER TERRIER

This is the smallest of the working terriers. It was bred in the middle of the 19th century to run with hounds and yet be small enough to bolt the fox from its lair.

COAT Harsh and dense with close undercoat.
COLOUR Red, wheaten, grizzle and tan, blue and tan.
FEATURES Dark eyes with keen expression; small V-shaped ears; deep, narrow, fairly long body; moderately short tail.
SIZE Height: about 25cm (10in). Weight: dogs 6–7kg (13–15½lb), bitches 5–6.5kg (11–14lb).
CARE Requires little grooming,
CHARACTER Makes a good pet. Usually loves all children, is long lived, will walk for miles and is a good watch dog.

CAIRN TERRIER

This popular Scottish terrier has been known and used for putting down vermin for 150 years. It was named after the cairns (a Scottish word for a mound of stones), which harboured vermin.

COAT Profuse, harsh but not coarse, with short, soft, close undercoat.
COLOUR Cream, wheaten, red, grey or nearly black; brindling acceptable.
FEATURES Small head; eyes set wide apart; small, pointed ears; level back; short, balanced tail.
SIZE Height: 24–30cm (9½in–12in). Weight: 6–7.5kg (13–16lb).
CARE Hardy and enjoys plenty of exercise. Needs little grooming except brushing, combing and removal of excess feathering.
CHARACTER Intelligent, lively, affectionate and effective for getting rid of vermin.

DANDIE DINMONT TERRIER

Believed to be related to both Skye and Scottish Terriers, this breed is named after a character in the novel *Guy Mannering* by Sir Walter Scott. It was bred to hunt badgers and foxes.

COAT Soft, linty undercoat, hard, non-wiry topcoat, feeling crisp to the hand.
COLOUR Pepper (from bluish black to pale silvery grey), or mustard (from reddish brown to pale fawn).
FEATURES Strongly made head, large but in proportion to dog's size; rich, dark-hazel eyes; pendulum ears; long, strong and flexible body; rather short tail.
SIZE Height at shoulders: 20–28cm (8–11in). Weight: 8–11kg (18–24lb).
CARE Happy with as much exercise as its owner is wishing to give it. Fairly simple to groom with a stiff brush and comb.
CHARACTER Intelligent, affectionate and playful.

WELSH TERRIER

The Welsh Terrier was once popular for hunting badgers, otter and foxes. Originally there were two strains – Celtic and English. Today's Welsh Terrier is descended from the Celtic strain, which used the old Black and Tan Terrier.

COAT Abundant, wiry, hard and close.
COLOUR Black and tan for preference; also black, grizzle and tan.
FEATURES Head flat and moderately wide between ears; small, dark eyes, well set in; small V-shaped ears carried forward; short, well ribbed-up body; muscular legs; tail well set on, customarily docked.
SIZE Maximum height at shoulders: 39cm (15½in). Weight: 9–10kg (20–22lb)
CARE Enjoys plenty of exercise and needs its coat stripped twice a year.
CHARACTER A fun dog, it is energetic, affectionate and good with children.

NORFOLK TERRIER

The Norfolk Terrier was originally classified as a Norwich Terrier, but gained official recognition as a separate breed in Britain in 1964, although not until 1979 in the United States. Both breeds originated in East Anglia in England and are a mixture of Cairn, Border and Irish Terriers. The only difference between the Norfolk and the Norwich today is their ears – the Norfolk has drop ears which fold forwards and the Norwich has alert, pricked ears.

COAT Hard, wiry and straight.
COLOUR All shades of red, wheaten, black and tan, or grizzle. White marks and patches undesirable in show dogs.

FEATURES Broad skull; deep-set, oval-shaped eyes; medium-sized, V-shaped ears, slightly rounded at tip and dropped forward; compact body.
SIZE Height at withers: about 25cm (10in). Weight: 5–5.5kg (11–12lb).
CARE Needs a lot of exercise. Requires daily brushing, and some trimming if to be exhibited.
CHARACTER A sociable, hardy and lovable dog. Despite being among the smallest of the terriers, it is alert and fearless, but good with children, with an even temperament. A good household pet.

NORWICH TERRIER

The Norwich Terrier is identical to the Norfolk Terrier except for the shape of its ears, which are alert and erect. Like the Norfolk, it originated in East Anglia and was very popular in the 19th century with undergraduates at Cambridge University. The breed's ancestors probably include Cairn, Border and Irish Terriers. The Norwich and Norfolk are traditional terrier breeds, well suited to hunting small prey in open terrain and with a tendency to disappear down rabbit holes when being taken for a walk.

COAT Hard, wiry and straight. Coat is rougher around the shoulders.
COLOUR All shades of red, wheaten, black and tan, or grizzle. White marks and patches undesirable in show dogs.
FEATURES Strong, wedge-shaped muzzle; small, dark, oval-shaped eyes; erect ears set well apart on top of skull; strong neck; short back; tail can be docked.
SIZE Height at withers: about 25cm (10in). Weight: 4.5–5.5kg (10–12lb).
CARE Enjoys regular exercise. Requires daily brushing, and some trimming if to be exhibited.
CHARACTER An adaptable, hardy and lovable dog. It is alert and fearless, but good with children, with an even temperament. A good household pet.

SKYE TERRIER

From the Isle of Skye, Scotland, it was originally developed to go to ground after badgers, foxes, otters and rabbits.

COAT Long, hard and straight with a short, close, soft woolly undercoat.
COLOUR Black, dark or light grey, fawn or cream, all with black points.
FEATURES Head and skull long and powerful; brown eyes; prick or drop ears; long, low body with level back.
SIZE Height at shoulders: dogs 25cm (10in), bitches 24cm (9½in). Weight: about 11.5kg (25lb).
CARE Magnificent long coat needs a considerable amount of grooming, especially as it loves country walks.
CHARACTER Tends to be rather suspicious of or uninterested in anyone other than its owner.

WEST HIGHLAND TERRIER

One of the most popular pure-bred dogs, the "Westie" was originally bred in the West Highlands of Scotland to hunt vermin.

COAT Harsh and free from curl, with a short, soft, close, furry undercoat.
COLOUR White.
FEATURES Slightly domed head; eyes set wide apart; small, erect ears, carried firmly; compact body with level back and broad, strong loins; tail about 15cm (6in) long.
SIZE Height: dogs about 28cm (11in), bitches about 25cm (10in). Weight: 7–10kg (15–22lb).
CARE Needs regular brushing to keep the white coat clean; stripping and trimming required for showing.
CHARACTER Plucky and hardy, gets on well with children.

SCOTTISH TERRIER

The Scottish Terrier, or "Scottie", was bred in Aberdeen, Scotland, purely as a vermin catcher.

COAT Sharp, dense and wiry with a short, dense, soft underfur.
COLOUR Black, wheaten, or any brindle.
FEATURES Head and skull long, but not out of proportion to the size of the dog; almond-shaped eyes; neat, fine-textured ears; moderate-length tail.
SIZE Height at withers: 25–28cm (10–11in). Weight: 8.5–10.5kg (19–23lb).
CARE Enjoys walks and ball games. Requires daily brushing. Its beard needs gentle brushing and combing, and its coat should be trimmed twice a year.
CHARACTER Playful and sporty, tends to be a one- or two-person dog. Reliable temper but doesn't welcome strangers.

SEALYHAM TERRIER

This breed can be traced back to 15th-century Wales, where it was bred for badger digging and hunting with hounds.

COAT Long, hard and wiry, with a weather-resistant undercoat.
COLOUR All white, or white with lemon, brown, blue or badger-pied markings on head and ears.
FEATURES Head slightly domed; dark, well-set eyes; medium-sized ears; medium-length body; tail carried erect.
SIZE Maximum height at shoulders: 31cm (12in). Weight: dogs about 9kg (20lb), bitches about 8kg (18lb).
CARE Needs regular brushing and must be hand-stripped if to be shown.
CHARACTER A fine show dog and family pet; good with children, but not averse to scrapping with other dogs.

CHIHUAHUA

YORKSHIRE TERRIER

The smallest dog in the world, the Chihuahua is named after a state in Mexico, and is believed by some to be a sacred dog of the Incas.

COAT Long coat: long and soft. Smooth coat: short, dense and soft.
COLOUR Any colour or mixture.
FEATURES Apple-domed head; large, flaring ears; large, round eyes; level back; high-set tail, curved over back.
SIZE Height: 16–20cm (6½– 8in). Weight: up to 2.5kg (6lb).
CARE Easy to groom, needing only daily combing and brushing.
CHARACTER Intelligent, affectionate and possessive. Has a lot of stamina and makes a good mini-watchdog.

One of the most popular Toy breeds, the "Yorkie" is a relatively recent breed, having been developed in Yorkshire, England, within the last 100 years.

COAT Glossy, fine and silky.
COLOUR Dark steel blue extending from back of head to root of tail; face, chest and feet rich, bright tan.
FEATURES Small head, flat on top; medium-sized, dark, sparkling eyes; small, erect V-shaped ears; compact body; tail usually docked to medium length.
SIZE Height: about 23cm (9in). Weight: not exceeding 3kg (7lb) if showing.
CARE Needs intricate show grooming.
CHARACTER Bossy, affectionate, lively and utterly fearless.

ENGLISH TOY TERRIER

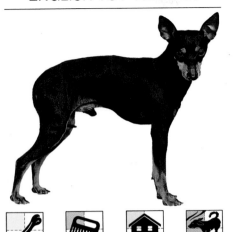

The English Toy Terrier, developed from the smallest specimens of Manchester Terriers, retains many of the bigger dog's working attributes.

COAT Thick, close and glossy.
COLOUR Black and tan.
FEATURES Long, narrow head; dark to black eyes; ears candle-flame shaped and slightly pointed at tips; compact body; tail thick at root and tapering to a point.
SIZE Height at shoulders: 25–30cm (10–12in) Weight: 2.5–4kg (6–9lb).
CARE Needs just a daily brushing and a rubbing to give its coat a sheen.
CHARACTER Rare outside the show ring; an affectionate and intelligent companion. Good with children but tends to be a one-person dog. Still retains its ability to hunt vermin.

LÖWCHEN

Also known as the Little Lion Dog, the Löwchen is a member of the bichon family and has been established in Spain and France since the 16th century.

COAT Moderately long and wavy.
COLOUR Any colour or combination.
FEATURES Wide, short skull; long pendant ears, well fringed; round, dark eyes, with intelligent expression; short, strong body; medium-length tail, often clipped to resemble a plume.
SIZE Height at withers: 25–33cm (10–13in). Weight: 3.5–8kg (8–18lb).
CARE Requires daily brushing. If exhibiting, seek advice on clipping.
CHARACTER Affectionate, intelligent and lively, popular in the show ring but rarely seen walking in the park. Enjoys life as a pet, given the opportunity.

BICHON FRISE

Similar in appearance to the Miniature Poodle, the Bichon Frise is thought to be a descendant of the French water dog, the Barbet; its name comes from the diminutive *barbichon*. Also known as the Tenerife Dog, it is said to have been introduced to Tenerife in the Canary Islands by sailors in the 14th century.

COAT Long and loosely curling.
COLOUR White, cream or apricot.
FEATURES Long ears, hanging close to head; dark, round eyes with black rims; relatively long, arched neck; tail carried gracefully curved over the body.
SIZE Height at withers: 23–28cm (9–11in). Weight: 3–6kg (7–13lb).
CARE Needs to have its coat regularly scissored and trimmed to achieve a desirable shape.
CHARACTER Happy, friendly and lively, makes an attractive and cuddly pet. Enjoys as much exercise as owners are willing to give it.

PUG

A scaled-down version of the Tibetan Mastiff, the Pug probably originated in China. It was brought into the Netherlands in the 1500s.

COAT Fine, smooth, short and glossy.
COLOUR Silver, apricot, fawn or black; black mask, ears and trace along back.
FEATURES Ears either rose or button; very large, dark eyes; short, thick-set body; tail set high and tightly curled over back.
SIZE Height: 25–28 (10–11in). Weight: 6.5–8kg (14–18lb).
CARE Requires only modest exercise but shouldn't be exerted in very hot weather. Daily grooming with a brush and a rub-down with a silk handkerchief will make its coat shine.
CHARACTER Happy and intelligent, good with children.

BRUSSELS GRIFFON

Once kept in 17th-century Brussels to catch vermin, it became a companion breed because of its character. In America and Britain it is exhibited with the smooth-coated Petit Brabançon.

COAT Brussels Griffon: harsh, wiry. Petit Brabançon: soft, smooth.
COLOUR Red, black or black and rich tan with white markings.
FEATURES Rounded head, wide between the ears; eyes dark and black rimmed; short, level back; tail, carried high, customarily docked short.
SIZE Height: 18–20cm (7–8in). Weight: 2–4.5kg (4½–10lb).
CARE Rough coat requires a lot of attention, but can be clipped.
CHARACTER Intelligent and cheerful, with terrier-like disposition.

POMERANIAN

A member of the spitz family from the Arctic Circle, which was imported into Britain from Germany about 100 years ago.

COAT Long, straight and harsh, with a soft, fluffy undercoat.
COLOUR All colours.
FEATURES Head and nose soft in outline; medium-sized eyes; small, erect ears; short back and compact body; tail set high, turned over back and carried flat.
SIZE Height: not exceeding 28cm (11in). Weight: 1–3kg (2–6½lb).
CARE Loves long walks. A fine show dog, if you have time to care for its double coat, which must be groomed with a stiff brush daily and needs regular trimming.
CHARACTER Lively, robust, affectionate and faithful, loves getting lots of attention. Good with children.

AFFENPINSCHER

From Germany, the Affenpinscher is the smallest of the pinschers and schnauzers and has a monkey-like appearance. It greatly resembles the Brussels Griffon.

COAT Rough and thick.
COLOUR Black or grey.
FEATURES Slightly undershot jaw; small, high-set ears, preferably erect; round, dark, sparkling eyes; short, straight back; high-set tail, docked in some countries.
SIZE Height: 24–28cm (9½–11in). Weight: 3–4kg (6½–9lb).
CARE Thick coat benefits from daily brushing.
CHARACTER Appealing and naturally untidy-looking, has a keen intelligence and is very affectionate. Makes a good watchdog and, terrier-like, enjoys rabbiting.

PAPILLON

The name Papillon, French for butterfly, comes from its erect ears. An identical drop-eared variety is known as the Phalène or "moth". Originating from Spain, it is said be a descendant of the 16th-century Dwarf Spaniel.

COAT Long, abundant, flowing and silky.
COLOUR White with patches of any colour except liver; black and white with tan in spots over eyes, inside ears, on cheeks and under root of tail.
FEATURES Head slightly rounded; large, erect ears; fairly long body; long, well-fringed tail.
SIZE Height at withers: 20–28cm (8–11in). Weight: 4–4.5kg (9–10lb).
CARE Needs a daily brushing to keep the coat shiny.
CHARACTER Intelligent, usually healthy and has proved an able contender in obedience competitions.

MALTESE

One of the oldest European breeds, the Maltese has existed on the island of Malta for centuries, but also found its way to China and the Philippines via traders.

COAT Long, straight and silky.
COLOUR White, slight lemon markings on ears permissible.
FEATURES Slightly rounded, broad skull; slightly tapered muzzle; long, well-feathered ears; oval eyes; compact body; long, plumed tail carried arched over back.
SIZE Height at withers: not exceeding 25cm (10in). Weight: 1.5–3kg (4–7lb
CARE Needs daily grooming.
CHARACTER Healthy, long-lived, happy, lovable and good with children.

ITALIAN GREYHOUND

There's little doubt that this is a descendant of the Greyhound – one of the most ancient breeds in the world. It is also known as the Piccolo Levriero Italiano.

COAT Short, fine and glossy.
COLOUR Black, blue, cream, fawn, red or white, or any of these broken with white; white broken with one of above colours.
FEATURES Long, flat and narrow skull; rose-shaped ears, large, expressive eyes; hare feet; low-set, long tail, carried low.
SIZE Height at withers: 32–38cm ($12\frac{1}{2}$–15in). Weight: 2.5–4.5kg ($5\frac{1}{2}$–10lb).
CARE Feels the cold and needs a warm coat in winter. Legs are easily broken. Easy to groom, a rub-down with a silk handkerchief makes the coat shine.
CHARACTER A sensitive little dog that, despite its delicate appearance, enjoys a fair amount of exercise.

PEKINGESE

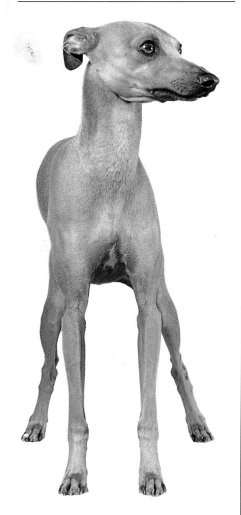

JAPANESE CHIN

For more than 1,000 years this dog was a favourite of Japanese emperors, who decreed that it should be worshipped.

COAT Profuse coat; long, soft and straight.
COLOUR White and black or white and red and white (all shades including sable, lemon and orange); never tricolour.
FEATURES Large, round head in proportion to size of dog; short muzzle; small ears, set wide apart; large dark eyes; square, compact body; well-feathered tail set high and curling over back.
SIZE Height:23cm (9in). Weight: 1.5–3kg (4–7lb).
CARE Requires an average amount of exercise and only daily brushing. Should not to be exerted in hot weather.
CHARACTER Affectionate, attractive and hardy little dog that is good with children.

Before the 1860s, Pekingese were only owned by the emperors of China.

COAT Long and straight, double-coated with coarse top coat, thick undercoat.
COLOUR All colours except albino or liver.
FEATURES Wide, flat head with shortened muzzle and deep stop; flat face; round eyes; feathered ears; thick chest and neck, short body with slightly rolling gait.
SIZE Height: 15–23cm (6–9in). Weight: 3–6kg (7–13lb).
CARE Requires considerable grooming.
CHARACTER Intelligent and fearless.

KING CHARLES SPANIEL

This breed's history can be traced back to Japan in 2,000BC.

COAT Long, silky, straight coat. Should only be slightly wavy for showing.
COLOUR Black and Tan (black with tan markings), Ruby (solid red), Blenheim (rich chestnut on white ground), Tricolour (black and white with tan).
FEATURES Large domed skull, full over eyes; deep, well-defined stop; low-set ears, long and well-feathered; wide, deep chest; well-feathered tail, carried above back.
SIZE Height: about 25cm (10in). Weight: 3.5–6.5kg (8–14lb).
CARE Needs brushing every day. Should keep the area around the eyes clean.
CHARACTER Friendly and obedient.

CAVALIER KING CHARLES

Like the King Charles Spaniel, the Cavalier originated in Japan and is similar in appearance to the Japanese Chin. It was a favourite of Charles II of England (1630–85).

COAT Long, silky, free from curl.
COLOUR Black and Tan (black with tan markings), Ruby (solid red), Blenheim (rich chestnut on white ground), Tricolour (black and white with tan markings).
FEATURES Flattish skull; long ears, set high; short-coupled body; well-feathered tail.
SIZE Height: 31–33cm (12–13in). Weight: 5.5–8kg (12–17lb).

AUSTRALIAN SILKY TERRIER

The Silky Terrier was originally known as the Sydney Silky. It was developed during the 1800s and is the result of cross-breeding between Skye and Yorkshire and Australian Terriers.

COAT Straight, fine, glossy.
COLOUR Blue and tan, grey, blue and tan with silver-blue top-knot. Tips of hairs should be darker than roots.
FEATURES Small, compactly built dog with body slightly longer than height; head medium length; eyes small, dark, round; ears small, V-shaped; tail usually docked.
SIZE Average height: 23cm (9in). Weight 3.5–4.5kg (8–10lb).
CARE Needs good daily walks and regular brushing and combing. Show dogs' coats need a lot of attention.
CHARACTER Typical terrier temperament – lively, loyal and makes a good guard.

CARE One of the largest toy dogs, this breed enjoys a fair amount of exercise and daily grooming with a bristle brush.
CHARACTER Obedient, good-natured and fond of children; makes an excellent family pet.

INDEX